The Fort Lauderdale Travel Guide

Uncover Hidden Gems with Insider Tips for Your Vacation in 2024 And Beyond

Rose Parkhill

GET ACCESS TO OTHER GUIDES FROM ME

DETAILS

NAME: _____

ADDRESS: _____

PHONE: _____

Fort Lauderdale, FL, USA.

HOW TO LOOK FOR DIRECTIONS

- Scan the QR-code to find the route to your destination.
- On google maps, click the button to choose the location and destination of your choice.

TABLE OF CONTENTS

INTRODUCTION

Welcome to the crown jewel of Florida's southeastern coast. Here, sun-kissed beaches, flowing waterways, and a lively culture make it the perfect place to go on holiday. This beautiful city is sometimes called the "Venice of America," because of its unique mix of natural beauty, modern luxury, and laid-back charm.

Even though city leaders are worried about too much growth, they have allowed many new hotels and high-rise buildings to open. Some locals and tourists who visit often worry that the sight of sailboats bobbing in the water near downtown will soon be gone. But Fort Lauderdale is still known as the sailing capital of the entire world, and the water attractions don't seem to be going anywhere.

Brief Overview

Fort Lauderdale is a busy city on the Atlantic coast, just 25 miles north of Miami. It feels like a beach town, even though it is a big city. Fort Lauderdale was named after Major William Lauderdale, who built it in 1838 during the Second Seminole War. It was founded in 1911 with only 175 people living there, but it multiplied during the Florida boom of the 1920s. In the 1960s, it became a famous place for spring break.

The city gets about 3,000 hours of sunshine a year, which makes it a great place to visit if you love being outside. About 180,000 people are living in Fort Lauderdale, but the city's draw goes far beyond its regular residents. Each year, millions of tourists come to the area to enjoy its clean beaches, world-class shops, and diverse food scene.

What Makes Fort Lauderdale Special?

Fort Lauderdale is famous for its 165 miles of waterways and canals and is slowly but surely rising the rankings of top beach resorts to the pleasure of its citizens. The city's beautiful beaches, with their powdery white sand and crystal-clear seas, are great for relaxing, swimming, or simply watching the world go by. For those who love the beach, Fort Lauderdale offers a variety of water sports, including diving, snorkeling, and paddleboarding. But Fort Lauderdale is more than just a beach getaway. It's a city with a rich cultural legacy, as shown by its bustling theater area, numerous art galleries, and a schedule packed with festivals and events.

What to Expect in This Guide

This guide is meant to be your ideal friend as you explore Fort Lauderdale. Inside, you'll discover thorough information on the major sites, hidden treasures, and must-do activities that will make your visit unforgettable. I'll show you the greatest locations to eat, stay, and experience local culture. You'll also get useful advice on when to come, how to get about, and how to make the most of your stay in this amazing city.

Prepare yourself to explore Fort Lauderdale, a place where lifelong memories are created!

CHAPTER 1

PLANNING YOUR VISIT

Getting to Fort Lauderdale

Fort Lauderdale is incredibly approachable, making it a top choice for tourists. There are many easy ways to travel to this well-known location, including by bus, rail, car, or airplane. These are the best ways to get to Fort Lauderdale:

By Plane: The most accessible airport for travelers is Fort Lauderdale/Hollywood International Airport (FLL), which is ideally situated two miles south of the city center. FLL serves as a hub for Spirit Airlines and other major airlines such as Delta, Virgin America, and JetBlue, providing a diverse selection of flight choices.

FLL is not only the nearest airport, but also one of the most convenient, having quick access from I-595, I-95, and US 1. The airport has nonstop flights from 55 locations in the United States, as well as international services to Canada, the Bahamas, the Caribbean, Mexico, and Latin America. FLL also boasts ample on-site and off-site parking, with free bus services running every 5-10 minutes to take people from the airport to the rental car center or parking areas. An additional reasonable choice for visitors coming from abroad is Miami International Airport (MIA), which is the busiest airport in the US and the biggest in South Florida. It is situated 30 miles south of Fort Lauderdale.

Serving over 80 flights to roughly 150 places worldwide, MIA is a major entry for foreign visitors. While MIA is distant from Fort Lauderdale, it has a wide range of airline choices and is readily accessible via the Dolphin Expressway. West Palm Beach International Airport (PBI) is another option, located 44 miles north of Greater Fort Lauderdale.

Though smaller than FLL and MIA, PBI handles around 6 million people each year and was chosen the third-best airport in the United States by Condé Nast Traveler readers. PBI is easily accessible by I-95 and the

Florida Turnpike, making it an ideal choice for northbound tourists.

By Bus: Greyhound offers bus service to Fort Lauderdale from across the country, with the main station situated downtown. Greyhound Express avoids intermediate stations in favor of quicker and more direct routes. Alternatively, RedCoach USA offers a luxury bus service with fewer people, more comfy seats, and features like Wi-Fi and electricity outlets, making it a top choice for those who value comfort during their trip.

Greyhound Location: 200 NW 22nd Avenue, 33311 FL, United States.

Contact: 1 800 231 2222

Red Coach Location: 320 Terminal Drive, 33315 FL, United States.

Contact: 1 877 733 0724, www.redcoachusa.co

By Car: Driving to Fort Lauderdale is simple, with major roads allowing easy access from all directions.

Along the eastern border of the city, I-95 runs north-south, linking Fort Lauderdale with Jacksonville, Miami, and West Palm Beach. To the west, the Florida Turnpike connects Homestead and the Florida Keys to the north, and Orlando to the south.

Additionally, I-595 and I-75 link Fort Lauderdale to towns in western Florida, such as Naples, Sarasota, and Tampa. The Greater Fort Lauderdale region, commonly known as Broward County, extends from Deerfield Beach to Hallandale on the east and from Parkland to Pembroke Pines on the west, making it simple to go about by car.

By Train: Amtrak provides rail service to Fort Lauderdale, including stations at Broward Boulevard near I-95 and the adjoining neighborhood of Hollywood. Both sites provide easy access to local bus services, cabs, and car rental choices, ensuring a quick transfer to your final stop.

Location: 3001 Hollywood Boulevard, 33021 FL, United States.

Contact: 1 800 872 7245

Best Times to Visit

The months of December to April are the best times to visit Fort Lauderdale. These six months are ideal if you wish to avoid the bitter winter cold since they provide bright, sunny days with temperatures between 58°F and 82°F. Since so many visitors from the north arrive in Fort Lauderdale at this time to take advantage of the wonderful weather, it is referred to as the peak season. You could thereby run into some crowds, but the stunning surroundings make it well worth it.

Although summer and fall provide warmer weather, they also carry the danger of hurricanes and the possibility of rain. If you're thinking of visiting during this period, particularly in the summer, remember to bring light clothes, a hat, an umbrella, and plenty of sunscreen. The official hurricane season lasts from June 1 to November 30. Travel insurance is also a good idea since unpredictable weather might force you to adjust your holiday plans.

Navigating the City

Driving is the most feasible way to get around Fort Lauderdale. Even with the vast network of canals in the city, driving is usually easier and quicker. Despite their appeal, the canals may be perplexing since streets close to the shore sometimes twist or finish at the sea.

Nonetheless, a large portion of the city has a consistent grid layout, which facilitates navigation, particularly when it is away from the Atlantic. You can always take a water taxi to go to your next downtown location if you're sick of driving. Furthermore, Fort Lauderdale may be readily reached by plane, since the Fort Lauderdale–Hollywood International Airport (FLL) is located just five miles south of the city's center.

You can also fly into Miami International Airport (MIA), which is approximately 30 miles south, or Palm Beach International Airport (PBI), which is about 45 miles north, with rental cars accessible at all three locations.

By Car & Taxi: If you want to see Fort Lauderdale and its neighboring areas, owning a car is a must. With "streets" oriented east-west and "avenues" oriented north-south, the city's grid layout facilitates driving. You may explore neighboring sites like Miami or West Palm Beach, each with its distinct vibe, with more flexibility when you have a vehicle.

At any of the regional airports, major vehicle rental companies are available. Conventional cabs offer an additional choice but are rather costly. Starting at $2.50, there is an extra $2.83 per mile for fares. You may hail a taxi on the street, at the airport, or over the phone. As an alternative, ride-hailing services like Uber and Lyft provide a more practical and affordable means of transportation.

By Bus & Trolley: The Sun Trolley has trips downtown, along the beach, and on Las Olas Boulevard; if your destination isn't close to a canal, you may want to consider using it. Except for the Beach Link and Las Olas Link lines, which charge $1 per trip or $3 for a day ticket, the majority of routes are free. Check Sun Trolley's Routes, timetables, and Fares page for specifics since operating hours and timetables are subject to change. The county is also served by the commuter buses operated by Broward County Transit. Children under the age of 17 and the elderly get a discounted fee of $2 for each trip. A $5-day ticket may be purchased, while longer-term passes that provide unlimited rides for the life of the pass cost $12 to $20.

By Water Taxi: Discover the city in a manner unlike any other thanks to Fort Lauderdale's extensive canals, which are a part of the Intracoastal Waterway that runs from the ocean to the Everglades. Water taxis travel the Intracoastal and the New River through downtown, making stops at fourteen locations, including the Margaritaville Hollywood Beach Resort. All-day-long access is available, but tickets are a little pricey — $28 for adults and $14 for children ages five to eleven. Seniors and active military people may get discounts, as can customers who are going after 5 p.m. Every day from 10 a.m. to 10 p.m., water taxis operate, with longer hours on Fridays and Saturdays. They leave every 25 to 35 minutes from each station.

By Train: The 2018 introduction of the Brightline rail system provides a handy option for anyone who would rather not drive. The train takes around 30 minutes to get from Fort Lauderdale to Miami, West Palm Beach, and West Palm Beach. Trains operate daily from around 5:10 a.m. to 12:50 a.m., leaving every one to three hours depending on the time of day. Ticket rates vary according to ticket class either Smart or Premium, route, and departure time, but they start at about $20 one-way.

By bicycle: If your trips are shorter, you may want to check out the Broward B-cycle bike-sharing program. Attractions like the Museum of Discovery and Science and Fort Lauderdale Beach Park are easily accessible from stations, which are well situated in well-liked districts like Central Beach and downtown. Renting a bike costs $5 for 30 minutes or $50 for the whole day.

CHAPTER 2

TOP ATTRACTIONS & ADVENTURES

Parks & Nature

In Fort Lauderdale, there is a lot of natural beauty to see. Let me take you on an inside look at some of Fort Lauderdale's must-see parks and nature sights that make the city stand out.

Hugh Taylor Birch State Park: Hugh Taylor Birch State Park is a 180-acre green space that provides a peaceful diversion from the rush of daily life while in the center of the city. This park is a secret gem, great for those looking to relax with various outdoor activities. You may have a relaxing picnic, go camping, have a refreshing swim, or explore the park's peaceful rivers by canoe or kayak.

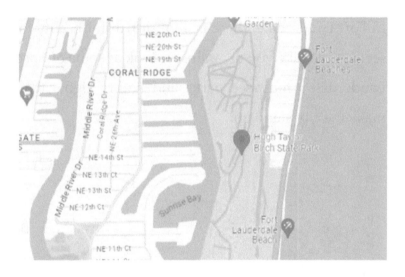

The park is also home to the historic house of Hugh Taylor Birch, the generous businessman who gave this beautiful land to the state of Florida. Walking around the park's pathways, you'll be enveloped in a panorama of mangroves, palm trees, and vistas of the Intracoastal Waterway. It is simple to combine your visit with other local attractions since the park has a water taxi station.

Location: 3109 E Sunrise Boulevard, 33304 FL, United States.

Contact: 1 954 564 4521

Fort Lauderdale Beach: It's easy to picture a perfect beach day, with long stretches of sandy shoreline lit up by the sun and the sound of gentle waves lapping against the shore. Fort Lauderdale Beach provides a peaceful vacation with all of the beauty of Miami Beach but in a calm, family-friendly atmosphere. The beach is known for having clean, calm water, which makes it a great place for families with kids. A famous feature that adds to the charm is the wavy white wall that separates the beach from the busy walkway. Although it costs $4 per hour, there is plenty of parking on the street, making Fort Lauderdale Beach an easy and friendly place to spend a peaceful day by the water.

Location: Florida A1A, 33304 FL, United States.

Butterfly World: The largest butterfly house on Earth is a wonderful place where you can lose yourself in a world of bright colors and flapping wings. This 3-acre attraction is a nature lover's and family's dream, with over 20,000 live butterflies and 50 different types. In addition, the park has a feeding area for lorikeets, where you can engage with these gregarious and colorful birds. Butterfly World was the idea of Ronald Boender, a passionate butterfly lover who built this haven to teach the public and protect butterfly homes. As you walk through the grounds, you'll be surrounded by the beauty and quiet of nature, making it a great spot for a peaceful afternoon. While outside food isn't allowed, there are picnic chairs and bars on-site where you can relax and enjoy a snack.

Location: Tradewinds Park - South, 3600 W Sample Road, 33073 FL, United States.

Contact: 1 954 977 4400

Flamingo Gardens: Flamingo Gardens is a 60-acre botanical park and Everglades wildlife destination located just 17 miles west of downtown Fort Lauderdale. As you walk through this beautiful oasis, you'll meet a diverse array of native Florida wildlife, from free peacocks to recovered Florida

panthers. With more than 3,000 different plant species living there, the gardens provide a vibrant and aromatic background for your stay. The guided tram trip through Flamingo Gardens' old oak trees and tropical forests is a highlight, providing a comprehensive overview of the park's flora and animals. This 25-minute trip is a must-do, and it's free of charge, going every 30 minutes.

Location: 3750 S Flamingo Road, Davie, 33330 FL, United States.

Contact: 1 954 473 2955

Fort Lauderdale Beach Park: Fort Lauderdale Beach Park is a good place for busy tourists, just a short distance from Las Olas Boulevard. You must find something to enjoy at the facilities, which include basketball and volleyball courts, outdoor showers,

 bathrooms, and a playground. The park's sands are often less busy than nearby beaches, offering a more relaxed setting for children. Lifeguards are on duty during daily hours, providing a safe setting for swimming. The park's closeness to stores, restaurants, and hotels adds to its appeal, allowing you to prolong your beach day into an evening of eating or shopping.

Just keep in mind that certain services, such as beach chair rentals, require an extra fee, and parking may be restricted, particularly on weekends and holidays.

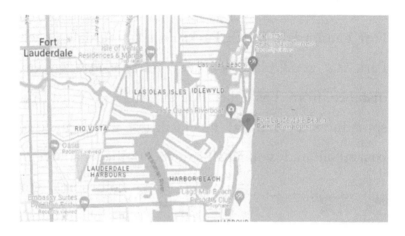

Location: 1100 Seabreeze Boulevard, 33316 FL, United States.

Contact: 1 954 828 7275

Las Olas Beach: Las Olas Beach is just north of Fort Lauderdale Beach Park. It has a lively scene, especially during Spring Break when it's a popular spot for college students. Even with so many people, the beach is kept clean, and sports equipment and beach chair and umbrella rentals make it simple to spend a day in the sun.

The beach is surrounded by restaurants, bars, and stores, so if you want to take a break from the ocean, there's plenty to do nearby. Police and park rangers walk along the beach to make sure it is safe for everyone who comes. Las Olas Beach is open daily from 6 a.m. to 9 p.m. and can be reached by car or public transportation, making it an ideal destination for a fun and active beach day.

Historic Sites & Museums

Under its colorful boulevards and palm-lined coastlines, there is a wealth of history that has molded this famous city. Imagine going back in time to an age of pioneer spirit, artistic energy, and amazing discovery. History isn't only in dusty books here; it's alive in beautifully maintained estates, lively streets, and interactive museums that entice you to take a trip through time. These are the top historical sites in Fort Lauderdale that provide an experience beyond the norm and have transformed the city into a lively exhibition of art, culture, and history:

History Fort Lauderdale: History Fort Lauderdale is home to three museums, each housed in one of the oldest houses in Broward County. The main attraction is the History Museum, housed in the 1905 New River Inn and detailing the development of the city from a modest fort during World War II to its current state as a thriving metropolis. The displays range from ancient times to the present, giving a thorough account of Fort Lauderdale's rich past.

Just a short walk away, the Pioneer House Museum provides a glimpse into early twentieth-century living, with rooms put up as if the family may return at any time. The family bedrooms with historical bed linens, Louise King's sewing room, and a children's room stocked with vintage toys and dolls are all upstairs.

The 1899 Schoolhouse Museum, complete with wooden chairs and old textbooks, takes you back to the days when education was a simple yet valued part of life. Together, these museums offer a fascinating trip through time, giving a better understanding of the people and events that made Fort Lauderdale into the city it is today.

Location: 231 SW 2nd Avenue, 33301 FL, United States.

Contact: 1 954 463 4431

Bonnet House Museum and Gardens: This 35-acre house on Fort Lauderdale Beach is a world where art, history, and nature combined. Entering the fanciful home will take you back to the 1920s when Chicago-born artist Frederic Clay Bartlett and his wife Evelyn Fortune Bartlett used it as their winter hideaway. Unlike the grandiose properties of the era, Bonnet House was intended as a personal refuge for the Bartletts, filled with private areas and artistic touches that reflect their creative spirits.

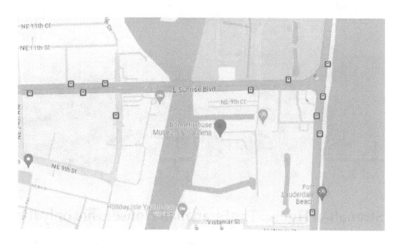

The house itself is a great trove of art, with walls adorned by Frederic's colorful paintings and Evelyn's delicate sculptures. Outside, the lush grounds are a quiet haven, where flowers grow and wildlife abounds. As you explore the grounds, you'll see that

Bonnet House is more than simply a museum; it's a living piece of history, wonderfully maintained in its 1930s and 1940s magnificence.

Location: 900 N Birch Road, 33304 FL, United States.

Contact: 1 954 563 5393

Stranahan House: The Stranahan House is not only the oldest surviving building in Fort Lauderdale, but it also serves as the historical cornerstone of the community. Built in 1901 by Frank Stranahan, Fort Lauderdale's founding father, this mansion has performed numerous functions throughout the years, including a trading post, post office, and community center. Aside from its utilitarian purposes, the Stranahan House was home to Frank and his wife, Ivy Cromartie Stranahan, Fort Lauderdale's first schoolteacher. With rooms that have been painstakingly restored to capture the period, a walk around the home today will give you an idea of what life was like at the turn of the century. The home is a testimony to the Stranahan family's important contributions to Fort Lauderdale's economic and social growth.

Location: 335 SE 6th Avenue, 33301 FL, United States.

Contact: 1 954 524 4736

Museum of Discovery and Science: This engaging museum is meant to spark wonder and ignite a love for learning in guests of all ages. MODS brings science to life, with hands-on STEM exhibitions and exhilarating animal experiences. Kids will enjoy exploring the Discovery Spot, which allows them to engage with Florida's distinctive landscapes, while the aviation-themed Makerspace provides a unique chance to be creative with flight-related crafts.

There are even more enjoyable and meaningful ways to interact with science outdoors at the Physics Science Park and Edible Food Forest. The museum is a location you'll want to visit again and again because of its constantly changing exhibitions, which guarantee there's always something new to discover. While the on-site meal options are limited, the museum's central position ensures that you're never far from other terrific culinary alternatives. It's simple and delightful to visit the Museum of Discovery and Science, especially with convenient parking just across the street.

Location: 401 SW 2nd Street, 33312 FL, United States.

Contact: 1 954 467 6637

Las Olas Boulevard: Las Olas Boulevard is the hub of Fort Lauderdale, combining history and contemporary to create a dynamic combination of culture and entertainment. As you walk along this lively avenue, you'll be surrounded by a colorful tapestry of stores, restaurants, and bars, each presenting a distinct flavor of the city. The street is home to some of Fort Lauderdale's most famous sites, including the historic Stranahan House Museum.

This place allows you to tour the early 20th-century house of Frank Stranahan, one of the founding fathers of Fort Lauderdale. The Riverwalk, another feature of Las Olas, invites you to take a relaxed stroll along the New River, where you can join a tango class, enjoy a lunch at Huizenga Plaza, or simply soak in the sights and sounds of the city. With over 30 al fresco eating choices, you'll never be far from a great meal or a cool drink.

Fun Activities

Fort Lauderdale has a wide range of activities to suit every taste and preference, from the exhilaration of pursuing a deep-sea fishing adventure to the calming appeal of an Everglades sunset. Here are some of the most fascinating ways to get the most out of your stay in this wonderful seaside destination:

Mini Powerboat Rental: Cruise through the beautiful rivers of Fort Lauderdale like a local with a small powerboat rental. Fort Lauderdale's complex canal system is lined with rich boats, opulent homes, and lush mangrove forests. With no previous fishing experience needed, you'll be at the helm of your small powerboat, exploring the waters at your own pace. This sport is ideal for taking in the views and sounds of the city from a different angle, regardless of whether you're in the mood for a leisurely ride or an exciting day on the water. Allow the soft waves to lead you through this breathtaking paradise as you kick back and unwind.

Half-Day Fishing Trip: This is your opportunity to catch the big one if you've ever wanted to go fishing in Fort Lauderdale for a half-day. With the stunning Fort Lauderdale shoreline as your background, picture yourself throwing a line into the crystal-clear blue seas. You'll pick up the fundamentals of drift fishing from the crew's knowledgeable advice, and maybe you'll catch a range of species including grouper, triggerfish, and amberjacks. The best part? Your catch will be cleaned and prepared by the crew for you to take home as a delectable memento of your journey.

Drift Fishing Trip off the Coast of Fort Lauderdale: If you're searching for a fishing trip that is a little more relaxed, think about going off the coast of Fort Lauderdale on a drift fishing excursion. This half-day trip takes you to the reef, just a mile away, where the waters are filled with snapper, grouper, and other reef fish. To give you the greatest opportunity to catch a fish, the knowledgeable team is available to assist with rigging and baiting. The team will clean your fish after a few hours of fishing so you can take it to a nearby restaurant and have it prepared to your exact specifications. It's a relaxing and satisfying way to spend a day on the water, with the plus of taking home a fresh, self-caught meal.

Champagne Sunset Cruise in Fort Lauderdale: Come onboard a cozy catamaran for a Champagne Sunset Cruise in Fort Lauderdale. As you glide by the opulent homes of Millionaires Row, let the soft sea wind carry you away. As the sun sets below the horizon, throwing a golden light over the Atlantic Ocean, raise a glass of champagne to cap off a magnificent day. This trip is a dream come true because of the romantic and pastoral setting, the graceful catamaran, and the breathtaking views of the coast.

One-Hour Airboat Ride and Nature Walk with Naturalist: This combo trip combines the greatest features of two tours into one: an exhilarating airboat ride over the Everglades and a serene nature walk conducted by an experienced naturalist. Starting your adventure with a walk through the park's several ecosystems will allow you to see alligators, birds, and towering cypress trees as well as hardwood hammocks and other species.

After that, take an airboat for an exciting voyage over the River of Grass, where you'll get the opportunity to see a remote Native tree island settlement. This tour provides a complete and memorable experience of the Everglades, mixing excitement with education and awe-inspiring natural beauty.

Fort Lauderdale Segway Tour: A Segway tour in Fort Lauderdale offers a fun and adventurous way to experience the city. On this guided trip, cruise through Fort Lauderdale's lively neighborhoods, along promenades beside the beach, and through the city's historic center. You may take a 5- or 10-mile circuit, or take an evening trip to see the city lit up at night. Your guide will regale you with intriguing anecdotes and insights about the history and evolution of the city as you sail by famous sites like the Broward Center for Performing Arts and the Fort Lauderdale Historical Society Museum. Enjoy the excitement of riding a Segway while seeing more of Fort Lauderdale in an enjoyable and environmentally responsible manner.

Everglades National Park Biologist-Led journey: For nature lovers, there's no better way to experience the unique environment of the Everglades than with a biologist-led journey. With this all-inclusive trip, you'll go far into the Everglades and cruise through the Ten Thousand Islands, passing manatees, dolphins, and an amazing array of avian species.

After an airboat journey into the River of Grass, where alligators lounge in the sun and the endangered Everglades snail kite hovers above, the experience continues. You'll also have the rare chance to visit a Native tree island town, reachable only by boat, giving a glimpse into the rich cultural past of the area. Anyone hoping to see Florida's natural landscape's untamed beauty must take this comprehensive trip.

Day Trips & Nearby Getaways

Fort Lauderdale is the ideal starting place for spectacular adventures, with beautiful Atlantic Ocean waves, lush national parks, and attractive coastal villages all nearby. To improve your Fort Lauderdale experience, here's a deeper look at some of the top day trips and local retreats:

West Palm Beach: For an exciting day out, West Palm Beach offers a perfect mix of beachside relaxing, shopping, and family-friendly activities. Walk down one of the city's lovely beaches to start your day off, where you may swim, sunbathe, or just take in the sights of the ocean. Kids will like the two water parks, Rapids Water Park and Calypso Bay Waterpark, where they may splash and play until they drop. These are great places to take family vacationers. For animal lovers, West Palm Beach is a great trove of wildlife experiences. For a close-up view of African wildlife, travel through Lion Country Safari or visit Manatee Lagoon to see these gentle giants in their native environment. A different opportunity to get up close and personal with a range of animals is provided by the Palm Beach Zoo, and all ages may have an instructive and entertaining experience at the South Florida Science Center and Aquarium.

The Everglades: This enormous national park is a great trove of unique ecosystems, from huge marshes to thick mangroves. Imagine floating around the park's canals on an airboat, the wind in your hair, keeping an eye out for alligators lazing in the sun. The Everglades is home to a diverse range of animals, and hiking paths provide some of the finest chances to see them in their natural setting. Take a relaxed stroll along the Anhinga Trail, a path that runs through a sawgrass swamp filled with birds and other creatures. For a more daring walk, the Mahogany Hammock Trail takes you through a green forest where you'll find the biggest live mahogany tree in the United States.

Big Cypress National Preserve: Located slightly to the north of the Everglades, this expansive marsh provides a closer personal encounter with Florida's breathtaking scenery while serving as a refuge for many animal species. Because of the preserve's isolated position, you're more likely to see animals up close, whether you're hiking, air boating, or driving a four-wheel-drive car.

The park's ranger-led tours are a fantastic opportunity to learn about the area's distinct ecosystems as well as the flora and creatures that live there. From birding to alligator spotting, Big Cypress offers endless chances for outdoor fun in a clean, untouched environment.

Biscayne Bay: This bustling bay, is a thriving aquatic paradise, only a short distance from Fort Lauderdale. Just picture diving or snorkeling while vibrant coral reefs brimming with exotic species in the pristine waters of Biscayne National Park. The park's barrier reefs are among the greatest in the area, providing intimate interactions with a variety of aquatic species.

If you want to remain dry, take a glass-bottom boat excursion and see the aquatic environment from above.

For a truly immersing experience, consider chartering a boat for a deep-sea fishing trip or take a kayak out to discover the secret bays and islands. Don't miss a visit to Elliot Key, the biggest island in the park, where you can walk, camp, or simply relax in this isolated paradise. Adams Key, with its natural beauty and camping spots, is another must-visit for a peaceful journey into nature.

Fort Myers Beach: For a change of view, head west to Fort Myers Beach, where the beautiful white sands and blue waves of the Gulf of Mexico await. You may spend a leisurely day by the water in this little seaside town whether you're kayaking along the beachfront or just sunbathing on the sand. Families will love this location because of the shallow, tranquil seas and plenty of kid-friendly activities. They may interact directly with stingrays at the Ostego Bay Marine

Science Center and discover more about the surrounding marine environment. You may also see these gentle creatures gliding over the warm waters of Manatee Park by taking a short journey there.

Key Largo: This island paradise is well-known for its breathtaking ocean vistas and relaxed atmosphere, yet it's just an hour's drive from Fort Lauderdale. Spend the day relaxing on the beaches or diving into the seas to explore the world-famous John Pennekamp Coral Reef State Park, which is home to spectacular coral reefs and marine life.

For a different type of adventure, kayak through the park's mangroves or see a play at Theater of the Sea, where dolphins and sea lions take center stage. If you're a diving lover, the underwater world of Key Largo Dry Rocks is a must-see, giving a unique experience beneath the waves. Sun protection is important, so don't forget to pack sunglasses, a hat, and plenty of sunscreen for a day in the Keys.

CHAPTER 3

WHERE TO EAT & DRINK

Top Restaurants

This once-charming fishing village has transformed into a thriving culinary destination where you can enjoy everything from fresh seafood to exotic cuisine. Fort Lauderdale offers an array of eating choices that are sure to please your taste buds. Here are some of the best spots to dine and drink in this seaside paradise:

Tinta: This restaurant is a must-visit if breakfast by the seaside is part of your ideal morning routine. With the choice to eat indoors or outside on the lovely oceanfront patio, this little restaurant provides a peaceful start to your day. As you drink your coffee and admire the breathtaking views, you'll be treated to a cuisine that highlights fresh, local products with a Latin twist. Tinta is the sister restaurant to the resort's expensive Mexican spot, Lona Cocina Tequileria, and it shares the same dedication to quality and taste.

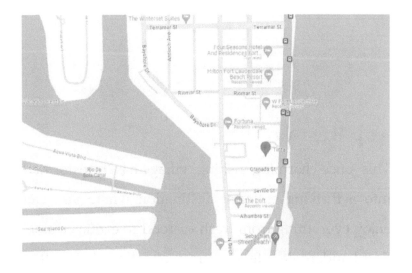

Location: 321 N Fort Lauderdale Beach Boulevard, 33304 FL, United States.

Contact: 1 954 245 3069

Coconuts: Coconuts is a spot where you can unwind, relax, and take in some of Fort Lauderdale's best views. With a prime location directly on the Intracoastal Waterway, this restaurant provides a special fusion of elegant dining in a laid-back coastal atmosphere. The environment is lively and comfortable, making it ideal for anything from a casual lunch to a romantic evening. The menu is a seafood lover's dream, featuring delicacies including coconut shrimp, crab cakes, and the well-known "Scoobies" (garlic crabs). The place is dog-friendly, and you can even come by boat, adding to the laid-back vibe.

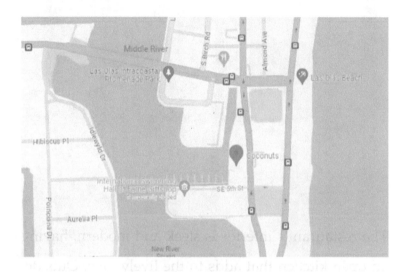

Location: 429 Seabreeze Boulevard, 33316 FL, United States.

Contact: 1 954 525 2421

YOLO (You Only Live Once): This restaurant's energetic environment and unique food mirror its name, which is a philosophy. Located in the heart of

Las Olas, this hip spot is where locals and tourists alike meet for great food, creative drinks, and a good time.

The restaurant's interior is sleek and modern, having an open kitchen that adds to the lively vibe. Outside, the patio is a great spot for people-watching while you enjoy meals like truffle fries, flatbreads, and fresh fish. YOLO is known for its expertly made modern American food, with a menu that changes seasonally to feature the best products. It's also a popular spot for happy hour and weekend brunch, making it a cornerstone of Fort Lauderdale's food and entertainment scene.

Location: 333 E Las Olas Boulevard, 33301 FL, United States.

Contact: 1 954 523 1000

Rustic Inn Crabhouse: This landmark restaurant began as a modest roadhouse saloon and has now evolved into a treasured institution, renowned for its outstanding garlic crabs. The environment is relaxed and friendly, with a focus on good food and good times. Because they love what they do, the staff members here will even take the time to demonstrate to you how to break open your crab for the finest possible dining experience. The Rustic Inn Crabhouse is a must-visit if you want to experience the authentic seafood scene in Fort Lauderdale.

Location: 4331 Anglers Avenue, 33312 FL, United States.

Contact: 1 954 842 2804

Casa D'Angelo Ristorante: When you enter Casa D'Angelo Ristorante, you'll swear you've been transported to a small, rustic Italian home. Renowned as one of Fort Lauderdale's best Italian restaurants, Casa D'Angelo is the creation of Chef Angelo Elia, who hails from Salerno, Italy. Every dish, from the exquisitely al dente pasta to the rich, delicious sauces, reflects his enthusiasm for real Italian cooking. The restaurant's setting is friendly and inviting, with an air of sophistication that makes it great for both private meals and big parties. Private dining rooms are available for individuals planning a special occasion, however, reservations are strongly advised to reserve your position at this popular eating establishment.

Location: 1201 N Federal Highway, 33304 FL, United States.

Contact: 1 954 564 1234

Steak 954: Steak 954 restaurant offers a polished atmosphere that's great for enjoying special events or simply indulging in a luxury meal. The restaurant's clean design, beautiful décor, and seaside views set the tone for an unforgettable dining experience. Together with an amazing assortment of seafood, the menu offers a choice of premium steaks that are all grilled to perfection. Begin your lunch with a seafood sampler that includes fresh oysters, lobster, and crab, then go on to a flawlessly cooked steak or twin lobster tails.

Location: 401 N Fort Lauderdale Beach Boulevard, 33304 FL, United States.

Contact: 1 954 414 8333

Sandbar Grill: With breathtaking views of the Atlantic Ocean and an extensive menu of traditional American dishes, this laid-back restaurant is situated on the beachfront terrace of the Sun Tower Hotel & Suites. The fish tacos are highly recommended, as are the beef burgers on pretzel buns, which are popular among locals. Sandbar Grill offers a variety of seating choices, ranging from open beachside tables to canopy-covered places, making it ideal for a supper by the sea. The seaside air, the sound of the waves, and the relaxed atmosphere make this a typical Fort Lauderdale dining experience.

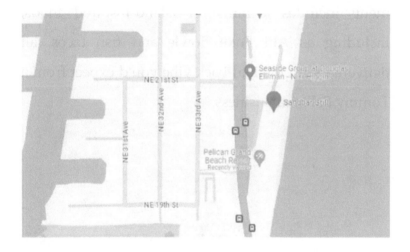

Location: 2030 N Atlantic Boulevard, 33305 FL, United States.

Contact: 1 954 565 5700

Tommy Bahama Marlin Bar & Store: Tommy Bahama Marlin Bar & Store is a laid-back haven in the center of Las Olas that lets you escape to the islands without ever leaving town. This casual spot is great for a quick bite or a relaxed afternoon with friends. The outdoor patio is self-seating, providing a laid-back setting where you can rest with a cold drink in hand. The menu includes a range of island-inspired foods, including as Ahi Poke Bowls and fish tacos, all delivered with the laid-back vibe you'd expect from a Tommy Bahama business.

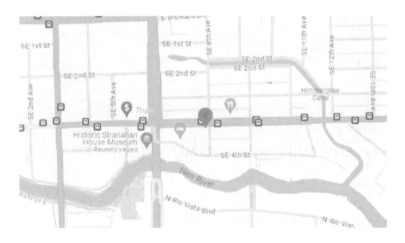

Location: 740 E Las Olas Boulevard, 33301 FL, United States.

Contact: 1 954 527 8868

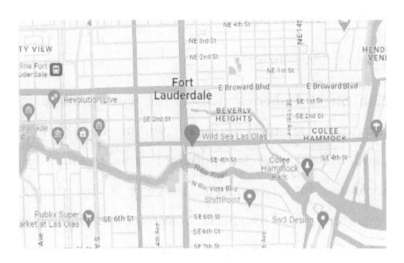

Wild Sea Las Olas: This lively restaurant is situated on Las Olas Boulevard and has a creative but accessible cuisine with meals that showcase the finest of the sea. The eating area is relaxed and friendly, making it an ideal spot for everything from a casual meal to a special event. If you want to people-watch, take a seat on the patio and enjoy your lunch outside while taking in the bright atmosphere of Las Olas. Wild Sea offers a delicious and unforgettable eating experience, with everything from fresh oysters to expertly grilled seafood.

Location: 620 E Las Olas Boulevard Riverside Hotel, 33301 FL, United States.

Contact: 1 954 467 2555

15th Street Fisheries: This classic Fort Lauderdale restaurant is tucked away within the historic Lauderdale Marina. This popular seafood restaurant is separated into two levels: above is a fine dining restaurant suited for special occasions, and below is a casual dockside eating space ideal for a laid-back dinner. As you eat, you'll be treated to amazing views of the Intracoastal Waterway, where boats and yachts cruise past. With items like stone crab claws, conch fritters, and the always-popular fish tacos, the menu is a celebration of fresh seafood. Don't miss the opportunity to feed the big tarpon from the marina's docks — this one-of-a-kind experience is popular with both residents and tourists.

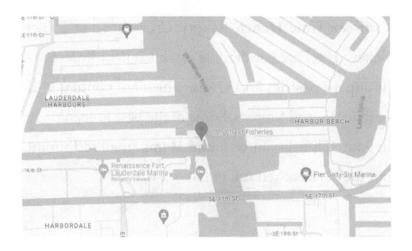

Location: 1900 SE 15th Street, FL 33316 FL, United States.

Contact: 1 954 763 2777

Coffee Shops and Cafes

The best way to start the day on vacation in Fort Lauderdale is with a perfectly made cup of coffee, and a cozy cafe is a great place to take a break from sightseeing. These places will make your stay in Fort Lauderdale better, from French bakeries that will take you to Paris to health-conscious restaurants that can accommodate special diets. Let's check out some of the city's best cafes:

Croissan'Time French Bakery: Croissan'Time French Bakery is a Fort Lauderdale establishment known for its superb pastries and bread, which are popular with both locals and tourists. Some of the best French treats in South Florida can be found at this small restaurant, but they are packed full of flavor.

The fluffy layers of the croissants are what make them stand out, but anything from their bread case is good. The baguettes are always warm from the oven and have a crisp outside and a soft inside. They are great for making a simple but filling sandwich. While the cooked foods may not be as good as the made goods, the staff's speed and the quality of the sweets more than make up for it. But be ready for a crowd—this spot is well-known for a reason.

Location: 1201 N Federal Highway 4A, 33304 FL, United States.

Contact: 1 954 565 8555

Fresh First: Fresh First is a South Florida restaurant and juice bar that is dedicated to providing wholesome, delectable meals that accommodate those with gluten sensitivity and other dietary requirements. It is the only establishment of its kind in the state. Tucked away in the yachting sector of Fort Lauderdale, this café serves up a cuisine full of healthy ingredients and vivid tastes. Since everything is cooked from scratch, each dish has the highest level of freshness. You'll feel satiated and invigorated whether you stop by for a small lunch, a substantial gluten-free breakfast, or a healthy smoothie. Fresh First is a new choice for those who want to keep a healthy lifestyle even while engaging in the food wonders of vacation.

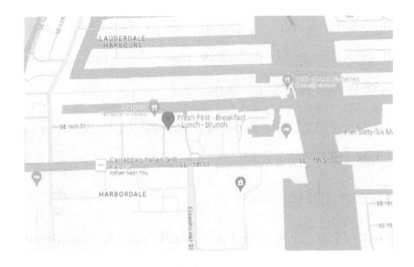

Location: 1637 SE 17th Street, 33316 FL, United States.

Contact: 1 954 763 3344

Cafe Ibiza: Picture yourself enjoying your morning coffee while feeling the soft touch of the ocean on your face and the sound of waves breaking in the distance. That's the experience you'll find at Cafe Ibiza, a charming beachfront spot that perfectly balances original tastes, warm kindness, and a welcoming setting. The menu includes fresh seafood, handmade pasta, and chilled salads, making it an excellent option for anyone seeking more than simply coffee. By night, Cafe Ibiza changes into a lively place with live music that goes nicely with a drink from the bar. Don't miss the fettuccini alfredo or the rich tiramisu—both are worth the splurge.

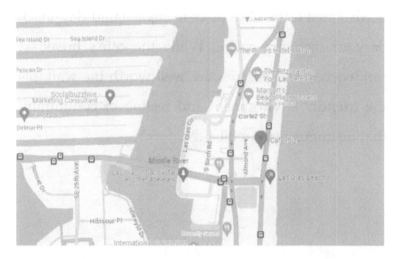

Location: 213 S Fort Lauderdale Beach Boulevard, 33316 FL, United States.

Contact: 1 954 468 9953

Archibald's Village Bakery: Archibald's Village Bakery is a community center that exudes warmth and kindness. It is tucked away in a quaint area and serves as more than simply a café. The aroma of freshly made pastries greets you as soon as you enter, and Chris, the proprietor, is always happy to see you. His Kent accent furthers the cafe's allure. With rich foliage and the sound of the neighborhood around you, the outdoor garden area is the ideal place to enjoy a mid-day snack or your morning coffee. While the cafe's breakfast sandwiches and pastries are well worth the wait, it's the friendly environment and feeling of community that distinguishes Archibald's.

Location: 608 Breakers Avenue, Suite 1, 33304 FL, United States.

Contact: 1 754 300 5926

Nanou Las Olas French Bakery: If you want a flavor of Paris in the heart of Fort Lauderdale, visit Nanou Las Olas. This beautiful, family-owned bakery serves a delicious range of freshly baked delicacies, including buttery croissants and luscious pain au chocolat. But the real highlight is the almond croissant, which is flaky, flavorful, and the ideal partner for their specialty coffee. The bakery's cozy, clean interior and closeness to the beach make it an ideal spot for a morning treat or a relaxed afternoon break. Grab a coffee and a pastry to go and relax by the lake, or use the free Wi-Fi to catch up on emails while indulging in delicious French delicacies.

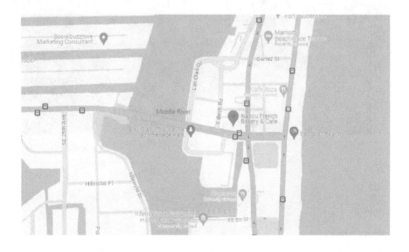

Location: 2915 E Las Olas Boulevard, 33316 FL, United States.

Contact: 1 954 616 8980

CHAPTER 4

WHERE TO STAY

Luxury Resorts and Hotels

Whether you're in Fort Lauderdale for a romantic break, a family holiday, or a single trip, you deserve a stay that fits the beauty of this coast city. Fort Lauderdale has a variety of luxurious places to stay to satisfy your need for comfort, style, and life-changing experiences, from lavish beachfront hotels to quiet boutique hideaways. Here are the best places to take a break, unwind, and feel better:

Conrad Fort Lauderdale Beach: This all-suite resort on the exclusive North Beach offers spectacular panoramic views of the Atlantic Ocean and Intracoastal Waterways from its 6th-floor Sky Deck and suites' private balconies. Each suite is an elegant refuge, complete with a superb kitchen, an Italian marble bathroom with a deep soaking tub and separate shower, and huge living rooms that will make you feel right at home. The Conrad is the pinnacle of understated elegance, with flawless service and mouthwatering food experiences to satisfy even the pickiest guest.

Location: 551 N Fort Lauderdale Beach Boulevard, 33304 FL, United States.

Contact: 1 855 618 4701

Premiere Hotel: This hotel is ideal for both single and family guests, only a short distance from the stunning Atlantic coastline. The environment is casual and pleasant, with a spacious swimming pool to unwind after a day on the beach. Guests often praise the hotel for its beautiful location, as it's close enough to Fort Lauderdale's main sights while still offering a quiet break from the noise and bustle. The Premiere Hotel stands out for its excellent value, giving reasonable rates with a range of free services, including food and beach gear. The staff here work hard to keep a friendly and welcoming environment, making your stay feel like a home away from home.

Location: 625 N Fort Lauderdale Beach Boulevard, 33304 FL, United States.

Contact: 1 954 566 7676

Hotel Hyatt Centric Las Olas Fort Lauderdale: The Hyatt Centric Las Olas is a place where the excitement of downtown Fort Lauderdale and the peace of a high-class getaway come together. This hotel is the right place to start your adventures in Fort Lauderdale because it is close to the city's best sights, shopping, eating, and nightlife.

The hotel's design was influenced by the nearby beaches. It uses soft ocean blues, neutral sand tones, and teakwood accents that look like they belong on a boat deck. The 238 rooms are built with luxury in mind, and they all have beautiful views of the pool deck and the city skyline. Harborwood Urban Kitchen and Bar serves modern American food with a global twist. Don't miss a meal there while you enjoy the lively atmosphere of Las Olas Boulevard.

Location: 100 E Las Olas Boulevard, 33301 FL, United States.

Contact: 1 954 320 0894

The Pillars Hotel & Club: This hotel is ideally located along the Intracoastal Waterway, just steps from the Atlantic Ocean. This elegant hotel is known for its excellent service, reminiscent of the best European inns. The hotel's setting is beautiful, with lush grounds and a quiet vibe that makes it a true escape from the outside world. Enjoying fine dining al fresco by the sea at The Pillars is a remarkable experience, particularly at The Secret Garden restaurant. The rooms and suites are beautifully arranged, giving a luxury and comfortable stay. Despite its peaceful surroundings, The Pillars is just a short walk from the beach and adjacent eateries, providing the ideal combination of privacy and accessibility.

Location: 111 North Birch Road, 33304 FL, United States.

Contact: 1 954 314 4269

Pelican Grand Beach Resort: This magnificent resort is right on the Atlantic Ocean, with amazing views and a peaceful, secluded beach. From the minute you arrive, you'll be fascinated by the resort's elegant architecture and warm atmosphere. The accommodations are nothing short of exquisite, with 156 rooms, including 106 beachfront suites with balconies from which you wake up to the calming sound of waves. The resort has the only Lazy River in Fort Lauderdale, which is ideal for a leisurely sundown float, as well as a lovely zero-entry pool that enhances the property's allure. Dining at Pelican Grand is an adventure in and of itself, with beachside choices offering exquisite meals and poolside cocktails with a view.

Location: 2000 North Ocean Boulevard, 33305 FL, United States.

Contact: 1 954 637 7187

W Fort Lauderdale: W Fort Lauderdale is a luxurious destination that combines the laid-back spirit of South Florida with its prime location on Fort Lauderdale Beach. This seaside hotel is a haven for those looking to absorb themselves in the beauty of the ocean, with rooms and services that are inspired by the peaceful blue hues of the nearby sea.

Excellent eating choices are available at The W, including the highly recommended Steak 954 and El Vez, where you can enjoy fine dining with a view of the ocean. The FIT gym provides a variety of fitness options, including beach boot camps and morning yoga classes. Afterward, treat yourself to a refreshing experience at the AWAY Spa, or simply rest in the Living Room with a perfectly made drink.

Location: 401 North Fort Lauderdale Beach Boulevard, 33304 FL, United States.

Contact: 1 844 631 0595

Renaissance Fort Lauderdale Marina Hotel: The Renaissance Fort Lauderdale Marina Hotel provides a contemporary take on coastal luxury and is located in the center of Fort Lauderdale's bustling Yachting area. This hotel is an excellent starting place for exploring the city, with convenient access to Fort Lauderdale

International Airport and the Sun Trolley, which connects you to the beach, Galleria Mall, and fashionable Las Olas Boulevard. The hotel's resort-style poolside cabanas provide a pleasant location to soak up the sun without paying an additional resort charge. The Renaissance also has R Lounge and Bistro 17, where you can enjoy regionally inspired meals and exclusive drinks in a sophisticated, relaxing atmosphere.

Location: 1617 SE 17th Street, 33316 FL, United States.

Contact: 1 844 631 0595

Hilton Fort Lauderdale Beach Resort: The Hilton Fort Lauderdale Beach Resort is a great choice for those seeking a seaside getaway with all the comforts of home. Every minute spent in your all-suite accommodation is a visual feast because to the breathtaking panoramic views of the Intracoastal Waterways and Atlantic Ocean. Each room is carefully built with a private patio, cozy sitting space, and either a pantry or a full kitchen, giving the perfect blend of luxury and ease. Take advantage of the 24-hour access to the exercise center, or simply relax on the ocean-view sun deck. The outdoor pool area is ringed by cozy cabanas, providing a private oasis where you can relax and soak up the Florida sunshine. One of the pleasures of your visit will be the Hilton staff's superb service, as they go above and beyond to make your stay as delightful and stress-free as possible.

Location: 505 N Fort Lauderdale Beach Boulevard, 33304 FL, United States.

Contact: 1 954 414 2222

Fort Lauderdale Marriott Harbor Beach Resort & Spa: This resort provides a secluded paradise with all the conveniences you want for a restful getaway, all situated along a quarter-mile of private beach. The rooms are intended to promote comfort and offer stunning views of the water, especially during sunrise.

While the location feels isolated and peaceful, the resort is still close to the energy of Las Olas Boulevard and the Fort Lauderdale airport. The resort features a variety of eating choices, from simple bites to fancy meals, all served with a side of stunning ocean views. The Marriott Harbor Beach crew is regarded for providing great service, making your stay as comfortable and pleasurable as possible.

Location: 3030 Holiday Drive, 33316 FL, United States.

Contact: 1 844 631 0595

The Westin Fort Lauderdale Beach Resort: The Westin Fort Lauderdale Beach Resort welcomes you to experience beachfront calm with a bit of modern luxury. The rooms are built with comfort in mind, having the famous Westin Heavenly Bed that ensures a good night's sleep. The resort's services are top-notch, with a 24-hour in-room eating selection, the Heavenly Spa by Westin, and a range of dining choices that cater to every taste. From Mexican cuisine at Lona Cocina Tequileria to a full breakfast at Tinta, the culinary experiences at The Westin are both fulfilling and unique.

Location: 321 N Fort Lauderdale Beach Boulevard, 33304 FL, United States.

Contact: 1 954 467 1111

B Ocean Resort Fort Lauderdale Beach: Built as the Yankee Clipper in 1956, B Ocean Resort on Fort Lauderdale Beach has a long history of being a favored hangout for famous Americans including Marilyn Monroe and Joe DiMaggio. Today, this sophisticated seaside resort continues to entice tourists with its ideal position on Fort Lauderdale Beach and its combination of historic charm and contemporary flair. The resort's 481 large, exquisitely designed rooms and suites have beach-chic décor drawn from the surrounding area. Guests may relax on the private beach, eat at one of the on-site restaurants, or see a unique mermaid performance at the world-famous Wreck Bar. B Ocean Resort provides a vibrant and memorable oceanfront experience, with facilities like two swimming pools, a 24-hour fitness center, and live underwater entertainment.

Location: 1140 Seabreeze Boulevard, 33316 FL, United States.

Contact: 1 954 787 3430

Budget-Friendly Accommodations

Sun-kissed beaches, bustling nightlife, and breathtaking waterways combine to make Fort Lauderdale the ideal destination for a vacation. However, you do not have to spend a lot of money to enjoy all this location has to offer. If you're seeking comfortable, reasonable hotels, Fort Lauderdale boasts a variety of options that don't sacrifice charm or convenience. Here are some outstanding selections that provide amazing value without sacrificing quality:

Marriott's BeachPlace Towers: Marriott's BeachPlace Towers provide a breathtaking view of the Atlantic Ocean from their balconies. With the convenience of being near all the excitement and the comforts and facilities of a Marriott hotel, this resort is perfectly situated only steps from the beach. The one- and two-bedroom holiday homes are great for families or groups, giving plenty of space and all the pleasures of home. When you're not relaxing on the beach, you may swim in the outdoor pool, eat at the poolside bar and restaurant, or exercise in the fitness facility. The cleanliness and care to detail at BeachPlace Towers are top-notch, ensuring a comfy and enjoyable stay.

Location: 21 S Fort Lauderdale Beach Boulevard, 33316 FL, United States.

Contact: 1 844 631 0595

Oasis Hotel: This small, boutique-style hotel is the perfect gem in the heart of Fort Lauderdale. The rooms include everything you need for a comfortable stay, including a flat-screen TV, air conditioning, and a refrigerator. The free Wi-Fi allows you to remain connected whether you're sharing holiday photographs or planning your next excursion. The Oasis Hotel is aptly named, with a calm sun deck and picnic area that invite you to rest after a day of traveling. The free parking is a big benefit, particularly if you intend on driving throughout the city. Located close to some of Fort Lauderdale's most famous buildings, you'll find it easy to involve yourself in the local culture and activities.

Location: 1200 Miami Road, 33316 FL, United States.

Contact: 1 954 523 3043

The Drift Hotel: This charming hotel provides a great combination of luxury and convenience for those who value charm and character. This boutique hotel is conveniently located near Fort Lauderdale's well-known beaches and bustling monuments, making it an excellent choice for exploring the city. The rooms at The Drift Hotel are built with your comfort in mind, having air conditioning, a flat-screen TV, and a microwave. The free Wi-Fi ensures you stay linked, while the fast check-in and check-out make your stay hassle-free. You may unwind and enjoy the Florida sun in this cozy setting created by the outdoor chairs and picnic area.

Location: 3005 Alhambra Street, 33304 FL, United States.

Contact: 1 954 774 2061

Riverside Hotel: The Riverside Hotel is the perfect alternative if you're looking for somewhere affordable to stay right in the middle of the action. This historic home, situated directly on Las Olas Boulevard, puts you in the heart of Fort Lauderdale's dynamic downtown environment. From the time you arrive, you'll be charmed by the Old Florida setting and the helpful, welcoming staff. The Riverside Hotel provides a unique combination of contemporary comfort and historic charm. The rooms are well-appointed, with stylish furniture and all the amenities you need for a peaceful stay. But it's the setting that truly shines. You're just minutes from the beach, the airport, and the boat port, making it a great choice whether you're in town for a short stay or a longer holiday. With multiple eating options on-site and open meeting areas, Riverside Hotel is as handy as it is lovely.

Location: 620 East Las Olas Boulevard, 33301 FL, United States.

Contact: 1 954 467 0671

Embassy Suites by Hilton Fort Lauderdale 17th Street: The Embassy Suites by Hilton Fort Lauderdale 17th Street is a great option if you are looking for large accommodation in a convenient location. This all-suite hotel is great for families, groups, and long stays, having a range of services that cater to your needs. The hotel is conveniently located near the Broward County Convention Center and Port Everglades cruise port, as well as Las Olas Boulevard, making it ideal for both leisure and business tourists. Every morning, enjoy a made-to-order breakfast, swim in the outdoor pool, or unwind with free drinks at the evening reception. The Embassy Suites offers a cozy and cheap stay with a bit of luxury.

Location: 1100 SE 17th Street, 33316 FL, United States.

Contact: 1 954 527 2700

Fortuna Hotel: The Fortuna Hotel is a cozy, reasonably priced hotel well-suited for both solitary and family guests. It is tucked away at a short distance from the beach. As the heart of the Gzella Collection, this small hotel is built with ease and convenience in mind.

The diversity of accommodation options assures that you will find something to meet your requirements, ranging from pleasant ordinary rooms to fully furnished apartments with kitchens. What sets Fortuna Hotel apart is the individual service. The staff is enthusiastic about making your stay special, giving expert tips, and helping you build a schedule that fits your interests.

Location: 350 North Birch Road, 33304 FL, United States.

Contact: 1 954 463 1723

Las Olas Guesthouse @15th Avenue: This guesthouse is conveniently located in a quiet area near Fort Lauderdale's attractions and beaches. This modern hotel is a true oasis, with services that match those of bigger locations but with a more private, personal touch. Each room is built for comfort, having Egyptian Cotton sheets, hot baths, and all the little luxuries that make you feel right at home. Start your day with a free morning breakfast, then rest by the pool or visit the nearby beaches and sites. Las Olas Guesthouse offers a peaceful getaway with all the comforts you need for a relaxing holiday.

Location: 908 NE 15th Avenue, 33304 FL, United States.

Contact: 1 954 683 6250

Neighborhoods to Stay In

Choosing the right area to stay can make all the difference in your vacation, with the finest of them having their uniqueness and appeal. As we explore each neighborhood, you'll locate the ideal location to suit your vacation style and make the most of your stay in this wonderful city.

Fort Lauderdale Beach: Fort Lauderdale Beach has the ideal balance of relaxation and thrills. making it a favorite among visitors seeking to unwind in luxury.

Imagine waking up to the sound of the waves lapping against the coast, the sun shining brilliantly, and setting off to explore one of the state's most stunning beaches. Just nearby, Hugh Taylor Birch State Park offers a green escape with hike tracks, a freshwater pond, and abundant wildlife. It's a nature lover's paradise, perfect for a morning stroll or a relaxing afternoon picnic. The activity is at Central Beach, which has palm trees bordering the flawless white sand, beachgoers soaking up the sun, and a variety of water activities to keep you engaged. After a day in the sun, stop by one of the neighboring beach bars or restaurants for a cool drink and a bite to eat while watching the sunset over the Atlantic.

Las Olas & Downtown: These areas are the center of the entertainment scene in the city. If you like being in the middle of the action, this is the place for you. Consider wandering along Las Olas Boulevard, which is lined with upscale stores, art galleries, and fine-dining restaurants. The atmosphere here is electrifying, particularly when the sun sets and the nightlife starts to thrive. Downtown Fort Lauderdale has several notable landmarks for individuals who like culture and history. Take a ride on a Water Taxi and explore the well-known canals of the city. It's an experience you won't want to miss, giving a unique view of the city from the water. As you glide past the Riverwalk walks along the New River, you'll see amazing boats that show the city's rich side.

Hollywood Beach: This area provides a more laid-back atmosphere and all the coastal beauty you'd expect from a Florida vacation, and it's located only south of Downtown Fort Lauderdale. The Hollywood Beach Broadwalk is a feature, running for 2.5 miles along the Atlantic coast. This pedestrian-friendly boardwalk is ideal for a morning jog, midday bike ride, or leisurely evening stroll. Along the journey, you'll come across several stores, cafés, and restaurants where you can get a bite to eat or have a drink while taking in the scenery. Hollywood Beach is special because of its dog-friendly area, where your pets may play in the sand and surf with you. Sky Beach Chair Rentals gives easy beach equipment rentals, so you can set up a comfy spot to spend the day.

Lauderdale-By-The-Sea: This little beach area feels like a step back in time and is just a short drive north of Fort Lauderdale Beach. This place is ideal for families or anybody wishing to get away from the bustle because of the slower pace and more laid-back atmosphere. The beaches at Lauderdale-By-The-Sea are breathtaking, with quiet, clear seas ideal for snorkeling and diving.

The area is famous for its colorful coral reefs, which are easily available from the beach, offering an underwater journey just steps from your towel. The main street of the neighborhood is lined with charming stores, welcoming cafés, and seafood eateries where you may savor the fresh catch of the day. The finest thing about Lauderdale-By-The-Sea is that it has managed to keep its old Florida charm, with buildings and streets that haven't altered much since the 1950s.

Flagler Village and Victoria Park: These two of Fort Lauderdale's hottest districts provide a blend of lively urban culture and laid-back charm. If you prefer visiting off-the-beaten-path locations, these are certainly worth considering.

Victoria Park is a peaceful, family area known for its lush grass and beautiful parks. Holiday Park is a favorite spot for parties, sports, and outdoor activities. Many of the area's restaurants welcome pets, and there's even a fantastic dog park where your four-legged buddy can get some exercise. Just across the highway, Flagler Village has turned into one of Fort Lauderdale's most exciting districts, with a lively street art scene, hip shops, and cool bars.

CHAPTER 5

CULTURAL INSIGHTS & LOCAL

LIFE

Annual Events & Festivals

Visitors from all over the world come to Fort Lauderdale for its multitude of celebrations and events. Fort Lauderdale's yearly events are more than simply dates on a calendar; they're the city's beating heart, with each giving a unique opportunity to discover and appreciate all this Florida treasure has to offer. Let's look at some of the most intriguing events to note on your calendar for your next visit:

Female Brew Fest: This one-of-a-kind celebration on September 14 honors the women creating waves in the brewing business, with over 15 brewers displaying their best products. As you taste a range of brews — from zesty IPAs to rich stouts — you'll have the opportunity to meet and learn from female brewers and beer specialists behind the scenes.

Viva Fort Lauderdale: Viva Fort Lauderdale is a celebration of Hispanic culture and art held from September to early October. This event is a cultural feast, giving a unique chance to meet with the local community and enjoy the variety that makes Fort Lauderdale so special. This party will fascinate your senses and leave you with a greater appreciation for the lively Hispanic influences that shape the city.

Wilton Manors Halloween Experience: Visit the Wilton Manors Halloween Experience on October 31 to celebrate Halloween like never before. Imagine a night filled with spooky fun, where the streets are alive with dressed people, lively activities, and vibrant nightlife. It's the best Halloween location in Fort Lauderdale, with a variety of bars, restaurants, and events to enjoy.

International Boat Show: Come to Fort Lauderdale from October 30 to November 3 and get ready to be astounded by the biggest in-water boat show in the world. This five-day event also features educational workshops, water performances, and a Superyacht Village, giving something for everyone.

Seminole Hard Rock Winterfest Boat Parade: The Seminole Hard Rock Winterfest Boat Parade on December 14 adds a tropical flavor to the holiday season charm. Known as the "Best Show on H20," this yearly show is a must-see. This 12-mile water procession is about more than simply the visual show; it is also about the vibe. With over a million onlookers gathered along the parade path, the excitement is obvious. Watching this floating carnival of lights beneath the starry Florida sky is simply lovely, and it makes for an amazing vacation experience.

Lauderdale Food & Wine Festival: The Lauderdale Food & Wine Festival is the event of the year from January 13-19. From new meals made by rising cooks to signature drinks mixed by master mixologists, this event is a celebration of flavor. It's not just about indulgence—this event also gives back, with a part of the proceeds helping Joe DiMaggio Children's Hospital. So, as you enjoy each delicious bite, know that you're also giving to a good cause.

Las Olas Art Fair: The Las Olas Art Fair is a dream come true with the famous Las Olas Boulevard, turned into an open-air gallery showing the work of skilled artists from around the country. The event takes place twice a year, so if you miss it in January, you can go again in March.

Pride Fort Lauderdale: Pride Fort Lauderdale is one of the major Pride festivities in the Southeast, bringing together colorful energy and love every February. Anticipate a weekend chock-full of LGBTQ+ community celebrations, art displays, and delectable cuisine. The happy mood is contagious, and the sense of community and cooperation will stay with you long after the event is over.

The Florida Renaissance Festival: This event brings history to life in the most exciting manner from

February 1 to March 22 (weekends only). Artisans show their homemade goods, from blown glass to finely tooled leather, while the smell of roasted meats and fresh bread fills the air. With heroes in shiny armor, fencing fights, and lively shows, this event is a lovely escape into a bygone era.

Tortuga Music Festival: This is a three-day festival from April 4-6, bringing together top names in country, rock, and roots music. This event aims to promote awareness of marine conservation in addition to offering fantastic music. So, while you're listening to music, you're also helping a good cause.

Las Olas Wine & Food Festival: On April 19, the Las Olas Wine & Food Festival will feature Fort Lauderdale's top chefs and restaurants showcasing their culinary abilities. This four-block street fair is more than simply food and wine; it's a celebration of the city's lively culinary culture, replete with live music and DJs creating the ideal atmosphere.

Fort Lauderdale Air Show: The Fort Lauderdale Air Show will provide an exciting experience from May 11-12. This event is a visual feast, with spectacular performances by the United States Air Force Thunderbirds and jaw-dropping feats by the Navy's Blue Angels. The air show takes place over the gorgeous background of Fort Lauderdale Beach and showcases a range of aircraft executing heart-pounding acrobatics.

The Stonewall Parade and Festival: Head to Wilton Manors in June to take part in this celebration of pride and equality. This yearly celebration, which attracts large audiences due to its exciting parade, live acts, and colorful street fair, is a highlight of the LGBTQ+ calendar.

The 4th of July Spectacular: Celebrate Independence Day in grand style at the 4th of July Spectacular, which takes place on Las Olas Boulevard. This free event is the ideal way to spend your summer vacation, with a joyful and celebratory setting evoking the spirit of Independence Day.

Experiencing Fort Lauderdale Like a Local

To properly experience Fort Lauderdale, you must travel beyond normal tourist sites, and to truly understand local culture, you have to lose yourself in the experiences that define the city. I'll highlight below several ways to get down and dirty in the center of Fort Lauderdale so you may experience the city like a native.

- Discover Fort Lauderdale's eclectic food culture, offering a wide range of delicacies to try. Locals know that some of the city's best places are found off the beaten path, away from the tourist crowds. Go beyond the main strip and seek out these culinary gems that highlight the finest of Fort Lauderdale's offerings if you want to get the full experience of the city.

- Fort Lauderdale's parks provide a peaceful break from city life, allowing you to interact with nature. In addition to being stunning, these parks provide as a glimpse into the more peaceful side of the city, where residents go to relax and take in the surrounding natural beauty. Spending time at Fort Lauderdale's parks allows you to calm down, breathe fresh air, and discover why so many people fall in love with our city.

- Taking a water taxi is an exciting way to see Fort Lauderdale. As you cruise, you'll pass by beautiful waterfront homes, and expensive boats, even spot some local wildlife along the way. The water cab stops at key spots like the beach, downtown, and the lively Las Olas Boulevard, making it a useful and beautiful way to get around. It's more than simply a means of getting about; it's an aquatic experience that presents a novel and captivating perspective on the beauty of the city.

- Visit Fort Lauderdale's famous beaches for a relaxing vacation. Whether you're enjoying the sun, cooling off in the sea, or trying out some thrilling water sports like jet skiing or parasailing, the beach is the ideal spot to relax. Wander down the beachside promenade as the day comes to an end. Its bustling bars and eateries make it the ideal place to have a casual meal or a sunset drink. The beach is more than just a place to unwind; it's where the city comes to life, with a diverse mix of residents and tourists enjoying all Fort Lauderdale's shoreline has to offer.

- Attending local events and celebrations is a great way to experience Fort Lauderdale's lively culture. These events are more than simply entertainment; they celebrate the city's varied community and rich legacy. Whether you're dancing to live music, trying gourmet food, or finding local crafts, these events offer a unique chance to experience Fort Lauderdale's culture directly.

CHAPTER 6

PRACTICAL TIPS FOR TRAVELERS

Safety & Health Tips

Fort Lauderdale has changed from being known for its wild spring break parties to being a more relaxed and family-friendly travel destination, but like with any city, you should always be alert and mindful of your surroundings. To make your vacation pleasurable and worry-free, consider the following vital safety and health advice:

- Although Fort Lauderdale is a relatively secure place, car burglaries are still a frequent problem. Make sure all of your windows are closed and always lock your car doors. You must never leave any valuables, especially electronics like computers and mobile phones, in your vehicle. Even little things, like spare change, should be kept out of sight to deter would-be burglars

- Important papers, such as your passport, identity, and travel insurance, should be kept in a safe place apart from the originals. In this manner, you have backups to help with replacement procedures if anything is lost or stolen.

- It's safest to travel in groups while going out at night, particularly if you're a woman and traveling during spring break. Though it's no longer the spring break destination it once was, Fort Lauderdale can still have exciting evenings, so it's best to exercise caution after dark. Steer clear of solo strolling, and exercise extra caution in the city's west, northwest, and southwest sections.

- The stunning beaches in Fort Lauderdale are a big appeal, but you need to take some safety measures as well. Swim close to a lifeguard who is on duty and always observe any posted cautions regarding the state of the water. In case of severe currents or other hazards in the water, this guarantees that assistance is nearby.

- You should educate yourself about the rules and culture of Fort Lauderdale before your vacation. It will be easier for you to manage social interactions and prevent any unintentional offenses if you are aware of and respectful of cultural standards. Share critical personal information with strangers with caution, particularly while you're in public.

Useful Local Contacts

Keep important local phone numbers close at hand for emergencies. Here are a few crucial contacts:

- Emergency Services: 911
- Broward County Health Department: 1 954 467 4700
- Broward General Medical Center: 1 954 355 4400
- North Broward Medical Center: 1 954 941 8300
- Fire Department: 1 954 828 6800

- Poison Control Center: 1 800 222 1222

- Broward Sheriff's Office: 1 954 765 4321

- Florida Highway Patrol: 1 954 934 1818

- Animal Services: 1 954 359 1313

- Post Office: 1 800 275 8777

- City of Fort Lauderdale: 1 954 828 8000

- Social Security: 1 800 772 1213

Essential Packing List

I've spent many weekends and summers exploring Fort Lauderdale, so I know precisely what's required for a trip there. I'm here to assist with items that are specific and do not have a travel timeframe.

- Clothes: tank tops, shorts, sundresses, jeans, bathing suits (at least 2), and loose clothes.

- Accessories: Hat, Bathing suit cover-up, sunglasses.

- Shoes: Walking shoes, sandals, wedges or heels, and shower shoes for camping.

- Specific Items: Beach towel, bug spray, sports sunscreen, facial sunscreen, waterproof mascara, camping chairs, theme park bag, chapstick, and beach bag.

Money Matters

You can better control your spending while visiting Fort Lauderdale if you are aware of the local currency and follow some money management advice. The following information will help you manage your money while having a great time:

Currency and Exchange: The US dollar (USD) is the official currency of the United States, including Fort Lauderdale. Even though the majority of transactions these days are done digitally, there are several currency exchange shops in Fort Lauderdale if you would rather carry cash or need to convert international money. Recall that there is never a completely fee-free currency conversion service — there is always a commission or other cost involved. Here are some locations where you may swap currencies:

- Doral Exchange

  Location: 2414 E Sunrise Boulevard, 33304 FL, United States.

  Contact: 1 754 206 4917

- Galleria Currency Exchange

  Location: 2414 E Sunrise Boulevard Kiosk T45, 33304 FL, United States.

  Contact: 1 754 206 4917

- La Paisa Money Transfer Inc.

  Location: 3905 Davie Boulevard, 33312 FL, United States.

  Contact: 1 954 792 3873

- Snap Money Exchange LLC

  Location: 1104 NW 6th Avenue, 33311 FL, United States.

  Contact: 1 754 333 0079

- Currency Global Exchange

  Location: 3200 N Federal Highway K4, 33306 FL, United States.

  Contact: 1 754 715 6081

Budgeting Tips: Visiting Fort Lauderdale doesn't have to be very expensive. You may have fun on your vacation without going over budget if you prepare well. The following useful advice can assist you in staying within your budget:

- Stay a Little Off the Beach: Prices for accommodation directly on the main beach might be high. Choose a motel or lodge a few streets away, where you can still stroll to the beach and restaurants at a more affordable price. A lot of these accommodations include apartment-style rooms with kitchens so you may prepare your meals.

- Make Some of Your Meals: Consider cooking part of your meals at your lodging to save your food expenses. Your everyday costs may be greatly decreased by cooking at "home" and food shopping locally.

- Benefit from Free Activities: There are many free or inexpensive things to do in Fort Lauderdale and the surrounding regions. Take advantage of free entry days to museums, explore state parks, or just spend your days relaxing on the beaches. With these choices, you may take in the area's natural beauty and rich culture without breaking the bank.

- Travel Off-Season: Summer and the holidays are usually when Fort Lauderdale experiences its peak season. If your schedule allows it, think about traveling in the off-season when costs for travel, lodging, and even activities are often lower. You will escape the crowds and enjoy the lovely weather that persists.

CONCLUSION

As you reach the end of this travel guide, you're now armed with everything you need to dive into the colorful, sun-soaked paradise that is Fort Lauderdale. From its clean beaches and busy boulevards to secret gems only the locals know, Fort Lauderdale offers a variety of experiences that cater to every type of tourist.

This city has something unique in store for you, but remember that the true charm of Fort Lauderdale isn't simply in its attractions or events—it's in the warm smiles of its residents, the gentle swing of its palm trees, and the infinite horizon where the ocean meets the sky. As you walk along Las Olas Boulevard, take a water taxi across the beautiful waters, or bask in the golden light of the evening sun, you will feel the spirit of this wonderful location soak into your soul.

So go ahead, take this guide with you, but let your interest lead the way. Discover new areas of the city, connect with its lively culture, and make memories that will last a lifetime. Fort Lauderdale is more than simply a tourist destination; it is a location that lingers with you long after you leave its beautiful beaches.

Your experience in Fort Lauderdale has just begun. Accept it, appreciate it, and, most importantly, enjoy every minute of your trip.

Safe

Travels!

MY TRAVEL
JOURNAL

PLACES VISITED

DATE:

LOCATION:

WEATHER:

HOW I GOT THERE:

RESTAURANT:

HOTEL:

WHAT I ATE:

THINGS I DID

FAVOURITE MEMORIES

MY TRAVEL
JOURNAL

DATE:

PLACES VISITED

LOCATION:

WEATHER:

HOW I GOT THERE:

RESTAURANT:

HOTEL:

WHAT I ATE:

THINGS I DID

FAVOURITE MEMORIES

MY TRAVEL
JOURNAL

DATE:

PLACES VISITED

LOCATION:

WEATHER:

HOW I GOT THERE:

RESTAURANT:

HOTEL:

WHAT I ATE:

THINGS I DID

FAVOURITE MEMORIES

MY TRAVEL
JOURNAL

PLACES VISITED

DATE:

LOCATION:

WEATHER:

HOW I GOT THERE:

RESTAURANT:

HOTEL:

WHAT I ATE:

THINGS I DID

FAVOURITE MEMORIES

MY TRAVEL
JOURNAL

PLACES VISITED

DATE:

LOCATION:

WEATHER:

HOW I GOT THERE:

RESTAURANT:

HOTEL:

WHAT I ATE:

THINGS I DID

FAVOURITE MEMORIES

Made in United States
Troutdale, OR
10/07/2024

23503275R10070